From Tree to Me

Andrew Einspruch

Contents

Trees

What would the world be like without trees?
Trees make our parks and forests beautiful.
Their branches give us shade. We make tissues,
newspapers, and postage stamps from trees. We
use wood from trees for firewood and for making
things like furniture.

A long time ago if you needed to make something out of wood, you found a tree that looked good and cut it down. Earth was covered with forests. People thought there would always be lots of trees.

But forests don't last forever. When forests are cut down, they grow back very slowly. Sometimes they don't grow back at all.

Some forests are protected. People aren't allowed to cut down trees in these forests. Other forests are managed by **timber workers**. These people decide which trees to cut down. Then they plant new ones in their place. By carefully managing forests, we can protect them and still get the wood we need.

A timber worker plants trees to make a new forest.

Wood From Forests

To get wood from a tree, you need to cut it down. Timber workers use chain saws to cut down trees. Trees can also be cut down using machines called **harvesters**. These machines grab, hold, and cut the trees. When the tree is down, its top and branches are cut off.

Harvesters cut down trees.

Job Log: Faller

A **faller** is a person who cuts down trees with a chain saw. Fallers do this work carefully so that no one gets hurt when the tree falls. They also make sure the tree does not damage other trees when it falls.

Out of the Forest

The cut trees are dragged out of the forest using a machine called a **skidder**. The trees skid along the ground behind this machine. The skidder hauls the trees to the road. Next the logs are loaded onto a truck. Then the logs are driven to a **sawmill**.

Skidders are used to move logs out of the forest.

Job Log: Loader Operator

A loader operator drives a **grapple loader**. This machine picks up the logs and loads them onto a truck. The loader operator makes sure the logs won't fall off the truck on the way to the sawmill.

At the Sawmill

Trees are cut into **lumber** at the sawmill. The logs are cut to a length that is easy to handle. Then the pieces are cut so they have four flat, straight sides. After the wood is cut, it is stacked and dried.

A saw cuts the log into flat boards.

Job Log: Sawyer

Sawyers work the equipment at the sawmill. They know how to get the best wood from the logs. Sawyers must be strong because they move and cut hundreds of logs each day.

Using Wood

After the wood is cut and dried, it is ready to use. Wood is used for making houses. It is also used for making furniture and musical instruments. Many people build things with wood as a hobby. They make dollhouses, birdhouses, and wooden toys.

This girl is helping her father make a birdhouse.

Job Log: Carpenter

A **carpenter** makes things with wood. Carpenters use hand tools such as saws and hammers. They also use power saws and electric drills.

Making an Instrument

Many musical instruments are made of wood. Guitars are made of wood. There are about 30 pieces of wood in a guitar.

To make a guitar, the pieces are cut into the right shape. Then the pieces are glued together. The guitar is sanded to make it smooth. Then the wood is sealed with varnish to make it last.

Sanding the guitar makes the wood smooth.

Job Log: Luthier

Making a guitar requires lots of skill. A **luthier** makes stringed instruments such as guitars. Luthiers must know how to use the tools that shape wood. They also need to know what kind of wood makes the best sounds.

Glossary

carpenter   someone who builds or repairs wooden houses or furniture

faller   someone who cuts down trees with a chain saw

grapple loader   a machine that loads logs onto trucks

harvester   a machine that cuts down trees

lumber   wood that has been cut into boards

luthier   a person who makes stringed instruments

sawmill   a place where logs are sawed into boards

sawyer   someone who works the machines in a sawmill

skidder   a machine that drags cut trees out of the forest

timber worker   a person who helps manage a forest so its trees can be used for lumber